QUESTIONING

The French Revolution

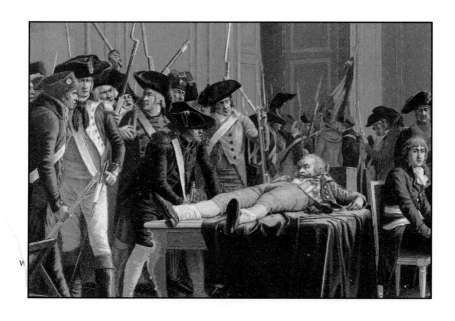

Nicola Barber

WAYLAND

© 2004 White-Thomson Publishing Ltd

Produced for Wayland by
White-Thomson Publishing Ltd
2/3 St Andrew's Place
Lewes BN7 1UP

Other titles in this series:
The African-American Slave Trade
The Arab-Israeli Conflict
The Causes of World War II
The Cold War
The Holocaust
Nazi Germany
The Western Front

Editor: Kelly Davis
Design: Chris Halls, Mind's Eye Design Ltd, Lewes
Consultant: Linda Kirk
Picture researcher: Kelly Davis
Proofreader: Felicity Watts

Published in Great Britain in 2004 by Wayland
A division of Hachette Children's Books
This paperback edition published by Wayland in 2008.

The right of Nicola Barber to be identified as the
author has been asserted by her in accordance
with the Copyright, Designs and Patents Act
1988.

British Library Cataloguing in Publication Data
Barber, Nicola
  The French Revolution. - (Questioning
  History) 1. France - History - Revolution,
  1789–1799 - Juvenile literature
  I. Title
  944'.04
ISBN 978 0 7502 5495 3

Printed in China

Wayland
A division of Hachette Children's Books
338 Euston Road, London NW1 3BH

Picture acknowledgements:

Mary Evans Picture Library 12, 13, 17 (Explorer
Archives), 18, 19, 23 (Auguste Couder), 26/27, 29
(Valentine Cameron Prinsep), 34, 35, 38
(Explorer Archives), 46, 48, 50, 52, 55 (James
Gillray), 56; Hodder Wayland Picture Library *title
page* & 47, 15 & 60, 24, 28, 36, 43 & 61, 53 & 60;
Peter Newark's Historical Pictures 4, 6 *left*
(Elisabeth Vigée-Lebrun), 6 *right* (A.F. Callet), 7
(Pierre Patel), 8, 10, 11, 16, 20, 22, 30, 32/33, 39 &
cover, 41 *above*, 41 *below*, 42, 44, 45 (Jacques-Louis
David), 49 (from a painting by Jean-Baptiste
Greuze), 51 (Baron François Gerard), 54, 59
(Eugène Delacroix).

Maps on pages 5 and 31 produced by Peter Bull.

Cover picture: King Louis XVI is executed
by guillotine on 21 January 1793.

CONTENTS

CHAPTER 1

France in the 1780s

THE EVE OF REVOLUTION

The population of France in the 1780s was around 28 million, of which about two-thirds was made up of peasant households. However, peasants owned only one-third of the land. The rest was owned by the nobility, the bourgeoisie and the Church. While a few peasant households had enough land to live comfortably, and owned their own animals and farming equipment, the vast majority of peasants held plots that were too small to support a family. Many rented extra land and borrowed animals and implements from richer neighbours who took a large share of their crops in return, a system known as *métayage* (share-cropping). Other peasants worked as tenant-farmers, and most took on additional work as labourers or textile workers to supplement their meagre incomes.

ABOVE *French peasants pay their taxes, while wealthy landowners look on. The inequality of the tax system was one of the root causes of the French Revolution.*

While Britain experienced an Agricultural Revolution during the eighteenth century, there was little improvement in agricultural techniques in France. Most landowners had little interest in such matters, and peasant farmers could not afford the time or financial investment needed to experiment with new farming methods. Nonetheless French farmers managed to feed an ever-growing population (which went up from about 21 million in 1700). Fear of hunger never went away, though, and in years when the crops failed, and the price of food rose, many people went hungry.

TOWNS AND CITIES

About 80 per cent of France's population lived in the country-side. However, compared to other European states in the eighteenth century, France had a high number of towns and cities, the largest being Paris, Lyon, Marseille, Bordeaux, Nantes, Lille, Rouen and Toulouse. Many of these places were commercial and manufacturing centres. For example, Lyon was famous for its silk weaving, while Nantes and Bordeaux both thrived on wealth from the slave trade between France, the Caribbean and West Africa (see page 40).

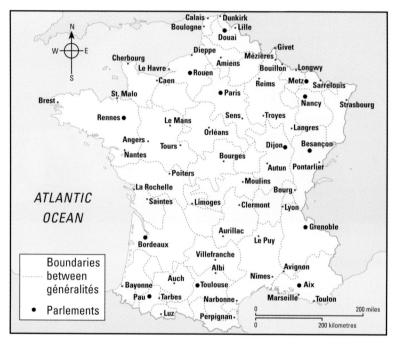

LEFT *Pre-revolutionary France was divided into 58 provinces which were grouped for administrative purposes into 33 regions called* généralités. *As you can see, the* généralités *varied hugely in size.*

? EVENT IN QUESTION

Were the bourgeoisie a threat to the nobility?

France's towns and cities were home to a middle class known as the bourgeoisie. These people had accumulated wealth (often through trade or business) but did not have the status associated with the nobility. Some were doctors and lawyers, some bankers, merchants or manufacturers, and many owned land. Some nobles saw the wealthy bourgeoisie as a considerable threat to their privileged existence. However, many of the bourgeoisie aspired to become nobles, often by buying offices which brought nobility after a generation or two. For this reason, most members of the bourgeoisie were unlikely to question the privileges of the aristocracy.

RIGHT *Louis XVI in his coronation robes, painted by A.F. Callet.*

ABOVE *Marie-Antoinette, Queen of France, painted by Elisabeth Vigée-Lebrun.*

ABSOLUTE MONARCHY

At the centre of the events of the French Revolution stood the king, Louis XVI, and his Austrian wife Marie-Antoinette. The two were married in 1770, four years before Louis succeeded his grandfather, Louis XV, to the throne of France. It took eight years for the couple to have their first child, a girl known as Madame Royale, but the longed-for heir to the throne (under Salic Law only male heirs could succeed to the French throne) was born in 1781. A second son was born in 1785.

Louis wished to be a popular king, but he had little first-hand knowledge of what life was like for most of his subjects. The court lived for much of the year at Versailles, a magnificent palace about 20 kilometres outside Paris, and sometimes moved to hunting palaces at Fontainebleau and Compiègne. Only rarely did the king visit Paris.

ALL-POWERFUL

Louis XVI was an absolute monarch. This meant that, although he took advice from his ministers, in all affairs of state the final decision was his. He was chosen by God as king of France, and he was answerable to no one but God for the wellbeing of his subjects. He appointed – and dismissed – the ministers and officials who ran the six departments of the state bureaucracy: finance, justice, foreign affairs, war, the navy and the royal household. In the hothouse atmosphere at Versailles, courtiers vied with each other for the king's favour.

Ministers who tried to introduce reform usually found that they had powerful enemies in the court. Appointed in 1774, finance minister Anne Robert Jacques Turgot undertook financial reforms and abolished guilds. He also attempted to reduce spending on the royal household. Louis sacked him in 1776. The same fate awaited another reforming finance minister, Jacques Necker (see page 11), a few years later.

ABOVE *The magnificent palace and grounds at Versailles, painted by Pierre Patel. Originally a hunting lodge, Versailles was built by Louis XVI's great-great-grandfather, Louis XIV, when he decided to move the court out of the Louvre in Paris.*

? PEOPLE IN QUESTION

Marie-Antoinette (1753–93): saint or sinner?

Marie-Antoinette was lively and extremely charming. She was also Austrian, the daughter of Empress Maria-Theresa, which made many people in France suspicious of her. She became a focus for all the gossip and intrigue in the royal court, and was a target of popular hatred from the outset of the Revolution. For the revolutionaries, Marie-Antoinette symbolized all that was wrong with their country. Yet after the Revolution she began to be depicted as a heroine and martyr. The truth probably lies somewhere in between. She was brought up in a glittering court and therefore knew little of life outside her privileged world. She had a sharp mind but little opportunity to use it. Yet she suffered her last years bravely, and met her end with great dignity (see page 45).

THE THREE ESTATES

Before the Revolution, French society was divided into three groups, or 'estates'. The First Estate was made up of the clergy, the Second Estate the nobility, and the Third Estate included everybody else from peasants to the bourgeoisie. The First and Second Estates accounted for about 500,000 clergy and nobles, and the Third Estate was made up of the remaining 27.5 million people in France.

BELOW *This contemporary illustration shows the Three Estates, represented by a priest (left), a nobleman (centre), and a member of the bourgeoisie (right).*

THE FIRST ESTATE

The Catholic Church was extremely powerful in France, and very wealthy. Many bishops and abbots lived in great luxury, drawing income from their lands and properties. However, most parish priests were poorly paid and overworked, and resented the wealth and arrogance of their superiors.

THE SECOND ESTATE

Nobles held the most powerful positions in the land, in the Church, in the armed forces, in the judiciary and in government. They did not pay any of the major direct taxes, because the *noblesse d'épée* (nobility of the sword) were supposed to pay their dues to their country by going to war when required. Families of the *noblesse d'épée* could often trace their lineage back over many generations. But a newer order of nobles, the *noblesse de robe* (nobility of the robe), had been created by the French kings, who had sold titles to ambitious officials and wealthy members of the bourgeoisie (see page 5).

THE THIRD ESTATE

In January 1789, a clergyman called Abbé Sieyès wrote a pamphlet entitled 'What is the Third Estate?'. It opened with the following words: 'What is the Third Estate? EVERYTHING. What has it been in the political order until now? NOTHING. What is it asking for? To become SOMETHING.' Sieyès went on to argue that the 27 million or so individuals of the Third Estate were actually the most important part of society in France, and that those who were not in the Third Estate could not consider themselves as 'belonging to the nation'. Such sentiments were increasingly popular on the eve of revolution in France.

> **? EVENT IN QUESTION**
>
> ### *Was there any common ground between the three estates?*
>
> Although the three estates are often discussed as if they were completely separate, there was clearly some common ground between them. For example, while a parish priest belonged to the First Estate, he often had more in common with members of the Third Estate, particularly in a growing dislike of the aristocratic bishops. Likewise, in the Second Estate there were some liberal nobles who agreed with many of the demands of the Third Estate. These reformers were often wealthy and well-educated, while poorer nobles tended to be more backward-looking and keener to protect the privileges of their estate.

TAXATION

One of the main causes of disagreement between the Three Estates was tax. While the First Estate owned about 10 per cent of all the land in France, it paid no direct taxes. Instead the Church paid a voluntary contribution to the government every five years. The nobles of the Second Estate were similarly excused from paying most direct taxes for historical reasons (see page 9), although a small tax on income had been imposed in 1749. It fell to the people of the Third Estate to pay taxes such as the *taille* (the major direct tax) and the *corvées* (taxes paid in service, such as laying and repairing roads). There were also indirect taxes, such as levies on salt (the *gabelle*), bread, alcohol and tobacco, as well as seigneurial dues (see page 12). As a result, the burden of tax fell on peasant households. The amount paid in tax varied hugely from region to region, and tax collection was often a haphazard affair.

RIGHT

'The Great Abuse' –
a peasant woman
supports the cruel
burden of the Church
and the aristocracy.

Jacques Necker (1732–1804)

After the dismissal of Turgot (see page 7), Jacques Necker was appointed by Louis XVI as director-general of finance. Necker did manage to cut expenditure on the royal household, but he argued against raising taxes. Instead he borrowed heavily, often at high rates of interest, in order to finance the American War of Independence. He also produced a set of accounts which gave a very optimistic view of France's financial situation. Some historians consider that the unjustified confidence created by Necker's accounts made any financial reform almost impossible, and helped bring France to a point of crisis which sparked the Revolution.

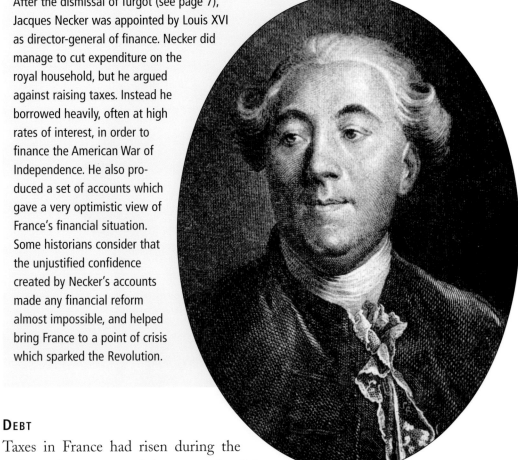

ABOVE *Jacques Necker, French statesman and financier.*

DEBT

Taxes in France had risen during the eighteenth century, mainly as a result of the need to pay for some very costly wars. The War of Austrian Succession (1740–48) and the Seven Years' War (1756–63) were both long conflicts that had ended in defeat and loss of territory for France. By the end of the Seven Years' War, France had a huge national debt, and successive finance ministers warned about the dangers of participating in any more wars. Nevertheless, France helped the Americans fight the British in the 1775–83 American War of Independence (see pages 16–17). The Americans and the French triumphed but the expense of the war sent France further into debt.

RIGHT *A prosperous seventeenth-century* seigneur *displays his wide-brimmed hat and fur-trimmed coat.*

Was resentment of the seigneurial system a major factor in sparking the Revolution?

In eighteenth-century France, most land was subject to the seigneurial system, a relic of medieval feudalism. This meant that the *seigneur* (lord) who owned the land had privileges, including hunting and shooting rights, the right to a pew in the local church, and the right to keep pigeons. *Seigneurs* controlled the local wine-press, flour mill and bread oven, as well as holding local courts. They could also impose charges on the peasants, either in the form of cash, or by demanding a share of their crops or other produce. During the second half of the eighteenth century, many *seigneurs* began to demand dues from their peasants more regularly than before. Although this caused resentment, most peasants accepted the system – until the bread shortages of 1789 triggered real unrest.

LAW AND GOVERNMENT

Pre-Revolution France was divided into 33 *généralités* (see page 5), each one governed by a minister appointed by the king, called an *intendant*. The *intendants* were responsible for government activity in their provinces, such as tax collection and public works. France was also divided into 13 judicial districts which, like the *généralités*, varied hugely in size. Each district had a high court, called a *parlement*. The magistrates who worked in these courts were the *noblesse de robe*, many of whom had bought the right to hereditary office from the king's government in previous generations. This meant that the only way to dismiss these magistrates was to repay the price of their office, which was impossible for the debt-ridden government.

The *parlements* were powerful for another reason too. Every law introduced by the king and his government had to be 'registered' by the courts before it came into force. The *parlements* could point out defects in the new laws by sending *remontrances* to the king. In theory, these *remontrances* were private documents, but during the eighteenth century increasing numbers were printed and published for public discussion. The king could choose either to ignore the *remontrance*, or to accept it and register the law with some changes. The king always had the power to enforce the original law, by appearing in person at the court in Paris (or being represented in the provinces by his *intendant*) to apply a forced registration – a process called a *lit de justice*.

THE ESTATES-GENERAL

From medieval times, there had been a representative assembly in France, known as the Estates-General. At this assembly, members of the Three Estates gathered to discuss legal and financial matters. However, the Estates-General did not meet regularly. Indeed when demands for an Estates-General began to grow in the 1780s, it had not been called since 1614.

BELOW *The playwright Pierre Beaumarchais (1732–99) questioned the rights of the* seigneur *in his comic play* The Marriage of Figaro. *The play was adapted by Lorenzo da Ponte for Mozart's opera of the same name.*

ELECTING THE ESTATES-GENERAL

When Jacques Necker resigned as director-general of finance in 1781, he was succeeded by Charles-Alexandre de Calonne. Like his predecessors, Calonne proposed a programme of reforms to try to improve French finances. However, he knew that his reforms would provoke opposition from the First and Second Estates, and from the *parlements*. He therefore called together the Assembly of Notables (a group of nobles, *intendants*, magistrates, clergy and others, all chosen by the king) to try to get backing for his plans.

The 144 members of the Assembly gathered in 1787, but Calonne failed to convince them. When the Paris *parlement* also refused to pass the reforms, calling instead for a meeting of the Estates-General, the king resorted to force. He had several leading magistrates arrested and the *parlements* suspended. In the summer of 1788 there were riots all over France, and the government finally ran out of money and credit. The king was forced to agree to a meeting of the Estates-General, and a date was eventually fixed for May 1789.

'DOUBLING OF THE THIRD'

The Estates-General had not met for over 170 years, and there was much discussion about what form it should take. Most of the clergy and nobility wanted to carry on the tradition of voting by order – that is the First, Second and Third Estates voting separately as three units. This would mean that the First and Second Estates could always outvote any reforms introduced by the Third Estate by two to one. However, many people started to call for voting by head rather than by order. In addition, there was a demand for the 'Doubling of the Third', doubling the number of members of the Third Estate so that their representation was roughly equal to that of the other two estates combined. The king gave way on this point, and about 600 members of the Third Estate were elected, equalling the 300 members in each of the First and Second Estates. But no decision was taken about voting procedures.

ABOVE *The meeting of the Assembly of Notables at Versailles, in February 1787.*

? ▌EVENT IN QUESTION

How important were the cahiers de doléances?

People across the country were invited to make lists of their grievances, called *cahiers de doléances*, which were taken to the meeting of the Estates-General in Versailles. At the meeting, all Three Estates expressed their loyalty to the king, and also agreed on the need for judicial reform, and, perhaps surprisingly, the need for concessions on taxation on the part of the nobility and the clergy. The *cahiers* cannot give a completely accurate picture of the French nation of the time – many of the concerns of the poorer participants were removed from the final versions. But they were important in making people think carefully about their grievances. They also raised expectations that something would be done to address these issues. However, such expectations remained unfulfilled.

CHAPTER 2

Ideas and Influences

THE AMERICAN REVOLUTION

In April 1775, the 13 British colonies in North America rose up against Great Britain after many years of what the colonists called 'taxation without representation'. (Although the British government imposed taxes on the colonists, the colonists had no representation in the British Parliament.) On 4 July 1776, the Second Continental Congress made a Declaration of Independence from Britain, and the United States of America was born.

ABOVE *This British cartoon of 1780 shows the French commander, Count Jean-Baptiste de Rochambeau, reviewing his troops in America.*

The fighting, however, continued. Several European powers, including France, formed alliances with the American colonists. France and America signed a treaty in February 1778, and French troops and warships reached American shores in 1780. The French played a vital role in defeating the British, surrounding the British general, Charles Cornwallis, at Yorktown in 1781, and forcing a British surrender. Finally a treaty, in which the British recognized the independence of the USA, was signed at Versailles in September 1783.

WHY DID FRANCE GO TO WAR?

The main motive for France's involvement in the American War of Independence was revenge. The French were still smarting from their defeat by Britain in the Seven Years' War (1756–63), which ended with the loss of French territories in North America, India, West Africa and the West Indies. The defeat also severely damaged French prestige, and left France with a huge war debt. The American War of Independence offered France the chance to recover some of its reputation, and to humiliate its old enemy – Britain. France was successful in both these aims, but the financial crisis sparked off by sending aid to America was one of the major factors that led to the French Revolution.

BELOW *Lafayette, then Commander of the National Guard, swearing an oath of allegiance to the king at the Fête de la Fédération in July 1790. The king in turn swore to uphold the constitution.*

? PEOPLE IN QUESTION

Marquis de Lafayette (1757–1834): revolutionary hero or traitor?

The Marquis de Lafayette took part in both the American and French revolutions. In 1777, he sailed to America with a group of other adventurers to help the American rebels. When France declared war on Britain, Lafayette returned home and was acclaimed a hero. He went back to America in 1780, and played a part in the victory at Yorktown. In France, Lafayette became associated with the cause of liberty, and helped to draft the Declaration of the Rights of Man (see page 27). In the early years of the Revolution, he took command of the National Guard, and later of one of the armies that went to war against Austria in 1792. But after he tried to protect the royal family during the attack on the Tuileries (see page 37), he became deeply unpopular with the revolutionaries. In despair at events in France, Lafayette fled across the border, only to be captured by the Austrians. He remained imprisoned until 1797.

THE ENLIGHTENMENT

The Enlightenment, which is also known as the Age of Reason, was an eighteenth-century philosophical movement, based on the scientific discoveries of the seventeenth century. Enlightenment philosophers used reason to challenge the traditional values of absolute monarchy, feudal society and established religion.

SCIENTIFIC ENQUIRY

During the seventeenth century, several scientific discoveries led to greater knowledge of the universe. In Italy, Galileo Galilei used mathematics and careful observation to prove Copernicus's theory that the Earth and planets orbit the Sun (as opposed to the previously accepted view, that the Sun and the planets revolved around the Earth). He also formulated new laws about motion. In England, Sir Isaac Newton used similar methods to draw up laws of motion and gravity, and to investigate light.

The philosophers of the eighteenth century brought a similar spirit of scientific enquiry to bear on Western society, law and justice. Their particular targets were the monarchy and the Church. In his essays *Two Treatises on Government* (1690), the English philosopher John Locke argued that people had the right to decide who governed them, and that if the government did not protect the rights of its citizens, the people had the right to change the government. Such Enlightenment ideas helped to shape the revolutions both in America and in France.

ABOVE *French philosopher and author Jean-Jacques Rousseau.*

THE PHILOSOPHES

The Enlightenment was largely driven by a group of thinkers known as the *philosophes*. They included Jean-Jacques Rousseau, François Marie Arouet (better known as Voltaire), Denis Diderot and Charles de Secondat (Baron de Montesquieu). These men had a variety of interests but shared a belief that existing systems of thought and government were harming people and limiting their capabilities. In general, they wanted to improve society through reason and tolerance.

ABOVE *Denis Diderot, teacher, translator and encyclopaedist, discusses his French encyclopaedia with his colleagues.*

? EVENT IN QUESTION

The English political system: a model of liberalism?

After the Glorious Revolution in England in 1688, the power of the English monarchy had been limited by Parliament. While much of the real power still lay in the hands of wealthy landowners, the liberalism of politics, religious worship and commerce was striking compared to the inequalities of French society. Voltaire spent three years in exile in England, and on his return to France wrote the *Philosophical Letters* (1734). In this book he used the English example to attack the French system, while still managing to poke fun at some of the shortcomings of the English political system. The book was banned in France, and Voltaire was forced to flee Paris. Nevertheless, the English edition, called *Letters Concerning the English Nation*, became a bestseller. Montesquieu also praised the English in *The Spirit of the Laws* (1748), particularly for their system of government.

Voltaire (1694–1778)

Voltaire was a successful playwright and a royal favourite – three of his plays were performed during Louis XV's wedding festivities. However in 1726 he challenged an aristocrat called Chevalier de Rohan to a duel after the Chevalier slighted him. As a result Voltaire was briefly imprisoned, and later exiled in England. There, the philosopher came into contact with the ideas of Sir Isaac Newton and John Locke (see page 18). On his return to France, Voltaire wrote many books, including *Candide*, a philosophical novel, which satirizes religious, philosophical and political systems (1759).

RIGHT *Voltaire, one of the best-known Enlightenment authors, believed passionately in religious tolerance.*

Jean-Jacques Rousseau (1712–78)

Rousseau wrote the single work that had the most influence upon the French Revolution. Called *The Social Contract* (1762) it began with the famous sentence: 'Man is born free but everywhere is in chains.' Rousseau was born in Geneva (now in Switzerland), and met a group of *philosophes* in Paris in the 1740s. He won fame in the 1750s through his writing, which explained that all legitimate power was derived from the people, and that when the people acted on an agreed moral basis they counted for more than any individual ruler or citizen. This idea of the 'general will' appears in the Declaration of the Rights of Man (see page 27), and came to dominate political argument between 1792 and 1795.

DENIS DIDEROT (1713–84)

Diderot was responsible for one of the most famous documents of the Enlightenment, the *Encyclopédie*. Diderot wrote on many subjects, and was influenced by the ideas of the English philosopher John Locke (see page 18). Like Voltaire, he was briefly imprisoned for his radical views, and one of his books, in which he openly attacked Christianity, was publicly burned in Paris. The *Encyclopédie* was published in volumes between 1752 and 1780, and it reflected the concerns of the *philosophes* throughout.

MONTESQUIEU (1689–1755)

Like Voltaire, Montesquieu lived in England for a short time, and looked to England for an example of good government. In *The Spirit of the Laws* (1748) he used the phrase 'checks and balances' to describe a system in which power is distributed as equally as possible. His theories were very influential when the American Constitution was drawn up in 1787.

? PEOPLE IN QUESTION

Rousseau: model for the wise?

Even before the Revolution started, there was a flourishing 'cult of Rousseau' in France, and his tomb was a shrine for his followers, both aristocratic and bourgeois. During the Revolution, Rousseau's ideas were used by the revolutionaries to justify many of their actions – including the mass killings of the Terror (see page 45) – and by aristocratic critics to condemn the Revolution. In the 1790s, during 'dechristianization' (see page 46) secular ceremonies were held which ended with a 'Hymn to Jean-Jacques Rousseau', including the words: 'Oh Rousseau, model for the wise, Benefactor of humanity'.

CHAPTER 3

The Revolution 1789–91

THE ESTATES-GENERAL

In late April 1789, the deputies of the Estates-General began to gather in Versailles. The Estates-General met on 4 May 1789 with a procession and Mass. Members of the First and Second Estates dressed according to their rank, while members of the Third Estate were obliged to wear black suits, stockings and cloaks, a reminder of their inferior status which many found difficult to accept.

The meetings that followed were mainly dominated by arguments over voting procedures. When the king refused to allow voting by head, the Third Estate also refused to work as a separate order and invited the other two Estates to join them. There followed weeks of inaction as the deputies argued. Then some clergy broke ranks and joined the Third Estate. On 17 June, the Third Estate declared itself to be a new representative body, known as the National Assembly. Many liberal noblemen and a large majority of the clergy soon joined the deputies of the new National Assembly. The Revolution had started.

BELOW *The Estates-General meets at Versailles in May 1789.*

ABOVE *The deputies hold their meeting in an indoor tennis court. Painting by Auguste Couder.*

THE TENNIS COURT OATH

In response to the action of the Third Estate, or the Commons as they had started to call themselves, the king decided to hold a special session on 23 June of all Three Estates. Until that time, Louis was determined that the so-called National Assembly should not meet, so when the deputies gathered on 20 June they found the doors of the hall locked. Undeterred, they gathered in the nearest large building, which was an indoor tennis court. Here, nearly every member of the National Assembly took an oath 'never to separate' until an acceptable constitution was established.

? WHAT IF...

the dauphin (crown prince) had not died when he did?

On 4 June, Louis XVI and Marie-Antoinette's elder son, the dauphin, died from tuberculosis. He was only seven, and although the boy's death was not unexpected his parents were devastated. The royal family left Versailles and went to Marly, a few kilometres away. The timing was crucial. At a point when the king's authority was being challenged on all sides, he was isolated from events and struck down by grief. If Louis had been able to stay in Versailles, and respond to the Commons without falling victim to hardliners' advice, he might have offered sufficient concessions early enough to have defused the anger that led to the declaration of the National Assembly. Some historians think the scheme he outlined on 23 June (see page 24) would have been acceptable if he had put it forward a few weeks earlier.

ABOVE *The storming of the Bastille, France's most notorious prison.*

THE FALL OF THE BASTILLE

On 23 June, the king met the Commons, nobles and clergy. Although he was prepared to make some modest reforms, Louis made it clear that the Three Estates and the seigneurial system would remain untouched. The Commons were not impressed, and over the following days more and more nobles and clergy joined the ranks of the National Assembly. On 27 June, Louis was forced to instruct the remaining members of the First and Second Estates to follow their fellow deputies. At the same time, he ordered troops to Paris and Versailles.

Across France, the people were becoming increasingly angry. After a disastrous harvest in 1788, food was in short supply, and the price of bread rose dramatically. There were outbreaks of violence in the countryside, and in Paris. However, the spark that finally ignited popular anger in Paris was the king's dismissal of his finance minister, Jacques Necker (see page 11). Necker had taken office for the second time in 1788, and was hugely popular with the French public. Under the influence of advisers who wanted to stop the Revolution by force, the king sacked Necker on 11 July. Three days later, on 14 July, an angry mob attacked the famous prison, the Bastille.

14 JULY 1789

On 14 July a crowd of 8,000 people laid siege to the prison. The governor initially refused to surrender, but when some of the troops began to side with the crowd, he gave in. The Bastille's handful of prisoners were released. And in the frenzy that followed, the governor and several of his guards were killed and had their heads hacked off and paraded before the mob. So began the violence that came to characterize the Revolution.

? EVENT IN QUESTION

Why the Bastille?

The Bastille was one of the most visible and oppressive symbols of the power of the state. But if the people of Paris hoped to release large numbers of prisoners from this grim fortress, they were to be disappointed – only seven captives staggered from the cells. However, there was a pressing need for arms, and it was also known that the Bastille was being used to store a large quantity of gunpowder. Whatever the reasons for the attack, the fall of the Bastille marked a turning point in the Revolution. The 'conquerors of the Bastille' were acclaimed as heroes, and in subsequent years 14 July was (and still is) marked with public celebrations. It removed the threat to the National Assembly, as the king was forced to take his troops out of Paris and recall Necker. It was also a symbolic victory for the people over royal power and absolutism.

THE GREAT FEAR

Across France, small revolutions occurred everywhere, as people refused to pay taxes and seigneurial dues. But rumour and suspicion reached even the most isolated areas during the summer of 1789, and people became fearful of revenge on the part of the nobles. This time of uncertainty became known as the 'Great Fear'. When it became clear that there was no plot for revenge, there were uprisings across France, with peasant anger mostly turned against the *seigneurs*.

In the face of this growing unrest, the National Assembly met on the night of 4 August. A proclamation calling for the restoration of public order was read. There then followed a meeting in which virtually all seigneurial rights were abolished. The writing up of these decisions took until 11 August, and many rights were in fact modified rather than removed. However, news of the meeting had already got out, and many in the countryside behaved as if the seigneurial system had been entirely abolished.

BELOW *The meeting of the National Assembly on 4 August 1789.*

THE RIGHTS OF MAN AND OF THE CITIZEN

On 26 August the National Assembly passed the 'Declaration of the Rights of Man and of the Citizen'. This document summarized the aims of the Revolution, and opened with the words: 'The Representatives of the French people, organised in National Assembly, considering that ignorance, forgetfulness, or contempt of the rights of man are the sole causes of public miseries and the corruption of governments, have resolved to set forth in a solemn declaration the natural, inalienable, and sacred rights of man...' It went on to list the 'rights of man and the citizen', the most important being that 'Men are born free and remain free and equal in rights.'

The Declaration of the Rights of Man promised the French people that they would no longer be the subjects of a monarch, but the citizens of a nation. The king, however, refused to accept the decree of 11 August or the Declaration. The stage was set for the next uprising of the Revolution.

? EVENT IN QUESTION

Did the Declaration address women's rights?

The Declaration was about 300 words long and could be printed on one piece of paper. It was read throughout France, and was used as the basis for the new French Constitution which was drawn up in 1791. But it contained some noticeable gaps, especially in relation to the rights of women. In 1791, an activist called Olympe de Gouges published her own 'Declaration of the Rights of Women and Citizenesses'. In it, she maintained that women were born free and equal in rights to men. She also pointed out that if women had the right to 'mount the scaffold' (be executed for their political beliefs) they should have the right to 'mount the tribune' (have a political voice) too.

ABOVE *Army officers enjoy a lavish banquet at the Opera House, Versailles, on 1 October 1789.*

BREAD RIOTS

On 29 September 1789, a new regiment of troops arrived at Versailles. As was customary, a banquet was given in the soldiers' honour at which the royal family made an appearance. Reports of this banquet, with many exaggerations, soon spread throughout Paris. These accounts, coinciding with another rise in bread prices, sparked off an angry response.

On 5 October a large crowd of mostly marketwomen collected in Paris, demanding bread. After storming into the Hotel de Ville, the furious crowd, now numbering about 6,000, began to march to Versailles. The National Guard set off after them.

The mob reached Versailles late in the afternoon and went straight to the National Assembly. Meanwhile the king's ministers advised him to flee while there was still time, but he refused. Eventually, six of the women were granted an audience with the king, who promised to provide them with bread. Later in the evening, Louis agreed to approve the National Assembly's decrees and the Declaration of the Rights of Man.

RETURN TO PARIS

The royal family went to bed, thinking that the immediate danger was over. However, a group of armed women came into the palace through an unlocked gate and broke into the queen's apartments. Just in time, Marie-Antoinette escaped into the king's apartments. When the women found that she had fled, they slashed her bed to ribbons. The women were cleared out of the palace, but it soon became clear that the mob would not leave without the royal family. Louis would have to return to Paris. The next afternoon, a grand procession including the royal family, the deputies of the National Assembly and, at the rear, the marketwomen, made its way to the capital. The royal family moved into the Tuileries palace.

? EVENT IN QUESTION

Women of the Revolution: at the centre of events or on the sidelines?

Women played an important part in revolutionary activity, and used the same radical arguments as men to argue for social and political justice. Many women from artisan and middle-class backgrounds were prepared to demonstrate on the streets. Women were accepted as members of some political clubs, such as the Fraternal Society of Citizens of both Sexes. There were also women activists who spoke out for the rights of women, including Olympe de Gouges, Théroigne de Méricourt, Etta Palm, Claire Lacombe and Pauline Léon. However, while thousands of women were active in the Revolution, the wording of the Declaration of the Rights of Man (see page 27) showed that there was no question of their being given the same rights as men.

ABOVE *The women of Paris march to Versailles (painted in 1894).*

NATIONAL ASSEMBLY 1789–91

Between 1789 and 1791, the deputies of the National Assembly worked extremely hard to reshape every aspect of politics and society in France. There were about 1,200 members of the National Assembly, and 31 different committees examined areas such as tax, weights and measures, government administration and the judiciary. The reforms introduced during this time shaped modern France.

ABOVE *A meeting of the National Assembly.*

ECONOMIC REFORM

In the Declaration of the Rights of Man, the National Assembly had stated that all French citizens had equal rights. Accordingly, the special privileges of the nobility were abolished in the decree of 11 August, and the Assembly announced that nobles and clergy would have to pay direct taxes to the state. The Assembly took several other measures to improve the country's financial situation. One was to ask for 'patriotic donations', another was the sale of Church lands (see page 31). A new tax system took longer to introduce, but from the beginning of 1791 tax payments were based on the value of property and the income gained from it.

RATIONALIZATION

Before the Revolution, many different weights and measures had been used in different regions of France. In 1790 the Academy of Sciences began work on the new standard measures, called the metric system, which eventually came into force in 1795. The administration of the country was also overhauled, and in 1790 the *généralités* were replaced with 83 *départements*, all of roughly similar size. The *départements* were divided into communes, the capital of each *département* being no more than one day's ride from any of its communes. The judicial system was similarly rationalized. Instead of the many different courts of the old regime, a new national system of courts was set up, with elected officers and citizens' juries.

LEFT *In 1790, France was reorganized into new administrative regions called départements.*

Church reform: a help or hindrance to the Revolution?

The Assembly put all Church lands and other assets 'at the disposal of the Nation', and much land was sold off to help solve the country's financial crisis. In return, the state funded the clergy out of public funds. The Assembly also decided to reorganize the Church, redrawing the boundaries of parishes, and proposing the election of priests and bishops by the people. On 27 November a decree was passed ordering the clergy to take an oath of revolutionary obedience. Most refused to do so, and became known as 'refractories'. The issue caused the first major split of the Revolution, between patriots who supported the reforms and those who opposed both the Revolution and its effects on the Church. Many historians see this as the point at which the Revolution became fatally divided.

CHAPTER 4

The End of the Monarchy 1791–93

FLIGHT TO VARENNES

While the National Assembly was busy reforming the government of France, the royal family were effectively captives in the palace at the Tuileries. In theory, the king could still appoint ministers and veto legislation, but in fact he had no real power. Although he appeared to accept the reforms to the Church, it soon became obvious that he was avoiding religious ceremonies which involved priests who had taken the oath of obedience. For the patriots of Paris, this was a serious matter and hostility towards the royal family grew. On 17 April 1791, a mob surrounded the royal carriage and prevented Louis and his family from going to Saint-Cloud, a small palace on the outskirts of Paris. Four days later, the royal family attempted to escape.

JOURNEY TO VARENNES, AND BACK

On the night of 20 June, the king, Marie-Antoinette and their children slipped out of the Tuileries palace in disguise and headed north-east out of Paris. Their destination was Montmédy on the border between France and Luxembourg. There, it was hoped that loyal troops backed by reinforcements

RIGHT *A contemporary print showing the arrest of the royal family at Varennes.*

from Marie-Antoinette's brother, Leopold II of Austria, would meet the royal party.

The alarm was raised in Paris on the morning of 21 June, and the capital was soon in uproar. Meanwhile the carriage carrying the royal family rumbled through the French countryside, reaching the town of Châlons at about 4 p.m., and then continuing to a village called Sainte-Menehould where the king was recognized. By the time they arrived in Varennes, news of the suspicious carriage and the king's flight had reached the townspeople. The carriage was stopped and they were forced, humiliatingly, to turn round and go back to Paris. Once they reached Paris, huge, silent crowds filled the Champs-Elysées. The royal family walked back into the Tuileries palace, now under heavy guard, and the National Assembly suspended the king from the exercise of royal power.

? WHAT IF...

the royal family had reached Montmédy?

The king's motives for the flight to Montmédy have been the subject of great controversy. Did he mean to leave the country and raise an army to end the Revolution by force? Or was he intending to stay in Montmédy, protected by loyal troops, and from there negotiate with the National Assembly? His motives will never be known, but it is true that certain deputies of the National Assembly welcomed the flight because they thought that it would be easier to reach a compromise with the king at a distance. One deputy wrote: 'if the king had got through, this great political crisis would have ended inside a month, with a good constitution and without a drop of blood being spilt.'

THE LEGISLATIVE ASSEMBLY 1791–92

The king's attempted escape to Montmédy fuelled growing popular distrust of the monarchy. While the royal family was on its way back to Paris from Varennes, a petition was drawn up and signed by 30,000 people in Paris, declaring that monarchy and liberty were incompatible.

Nevertheless, the majority of the National Assembly wanted Louis XVI to remain as king. When the Assembly announced its decision to reinstate the king another petition was organized, declaring the Assembly's decision contrary to the will of the people. Thousands of people gathered at the Champs-de-Mars, on the outskirts of Paris, to sign the petition. But the National Guard opened fire on the demonstrators and at least 50 people were killed.

BELOW *Louis XVI finally accepts the Constitution on 14 September 1791.*

THE CONSTITUTION

A condition of the king's reinstatement was that he would pass the Constitution, which was the outcome of the National Assembly's work since 1789. Accordingly, the Constitution came into effect on 14 September 1791. The National Assembly was dissolved and a new Legislative Assembly was elected, made up of new deputies. Its first meeting was held on 1 October 1791.

ÉMIGRÉS

Immediately, the Legislative Assembly had to deal with a pressing problem – the threat from outside France. Since the fall of the Bastille, many aristocrats, including the king's own brothers, had gone abroad. There was great suspicion in France that these émigrés were plotting against the government. In the autumn of 1791, thousands of French army officers gathered in Germany, where the king's brothers were based. They dreamed of overthrowing the Revolution with the help of foreign armies. In August 1791, the Emperor of Austria, Leopold II (Marie-Antoinette's brother), and the King of Prussia (a former German kingdom) had threatened military intervention on behalf of Louis XVI in the Declaration of Pillnitz, although no action was taken. On 20 April of the following year, 1792, France declared war on Austria.

ABOVE *A contemporary engraving showing Emperor Leopold II (1747–92) in his imperial robes.*

? EVENT IN QUESTION

How serious was the threat to France?

Fear of foreign aggression and the plots of the émigrés led the Assembly to take increasingly drastic action during 1791. Decrees were issued, demanding the return of the émigrés, promising death for conspirators against the state, confiscating émigrés' land, and stripping the Comte de Provence, brother of Louis XVI, of the right to succeed to the French throne. The threat was serious enough, but the king's reaction was equally destabilizing. Not surprisingly, he vetoed many of the decrees, adding to suspicions that he was involved in plots against his own government and fuelling the growing antagonism towards him.

ABOVE *A family celebrates the march of the* féderés *by singing 'The Marseillaise', which is still the national anthem of France.*

THE FÉDERÉS AND THE SANS-CULOTTES

The war began very badly for the French. Thousands of French army officers had left France (see page 35), and the army was in disarray. Prussia and Austria together invaded France, heading for Paris. The Assembly then called up thousands of volunteers, called *féderés*, to defend the capital and they began to arrive from all over the country. On 1 August, the *féderés* from Marseille marched into Paris, to a song known as 'The Marseillaise' in their honour.

Another militant revolutionary group was the *sans-culottes*, a term meaning 'without breeches' (referring to the fact that wealthy men wore knee breeches, while ordinary workers wore trousers). The *sans-culottes* were mostly craftsmen, shopkeepers and labourers, and they became very powerful as the Revolution progressed.

THE OVERTHROW OF THE MONARCHY

On 25 July, the commander of the Prussian army, the Duke of Brunswick, threatened the 'total destruction' of Paris if the royal family was harmed (a threat which confirmed popular belief that the king was conspiring with foreign powers). On 10 August, a huge crowd attacked the Tuileries palace, forcing the royal family to take refuge with the Legislative Assembly. The Assembly suspended the monarchy and decided that a new body, called the National Convention, should be elected. The monarchy was overthrown and the royal family imprisoned.

THE SEPTEMBER MASSACRES

Meanwhile the war continued. On 1 September, the Prussians captured Verdun, about 250 km north-east of Paris, and this news caused uproar in the capital. The prisons in Paris were full of 'counter-revolutionaries' – nobles, priests and others who had opposed the Revolution – and a fear grew that these prisoners would seize the opportunity to break out and take revenge on the population before welcoming the Prussian invaders. In the atmosphere of rumour and fear, some counter-revolutionaries were tried by improvised courts and more than a thousand were put to death – often with no trial at all. Many others were released. The killings came to be known as the September Massacres.

The journalist Jean-Paul Marat urged people in the provinces to follow the example of Paris, but people both in France and abroad were horrified by the killings. The massacres cast a shadow over the first meeting of the National Convention on 20 September. However, the same day brought better news from the war – a French victory against the Prussians at Valmy.

? PEOPLE IN QUESTION

Jean-Paul Marat (1743–93): martyr or monster?

Jean-Paul Marat edited a paper called *L'Ami du peuple* ('The people's friend'). He encouraged the September Massacres and called for the execution of all opponents of the Revolution. His extremist views made him hugely popular with ordinary people, and he was elected to represent the people of Paris in the National Convention. However, at the peak of his powers he was murdered (see page 43), and instantly became a revolutionary martyr.

THE CASE AGAINST THE KING

The first act of the National Convention, on 21 September, was to abolish the monarchy and declare France a republic. The Convention also voted to introduce a new revolutionary calendar. But the most pressing question was what to do with the king. Some deputies, including Jean-Paul Marat and Maximilien Robespierre, argued that he should be executed for treason straight away; others believed that he should stand trial. The case was strengthened by the discovery of a huge iron box hidden behind a wall in the Tuileries palace. It was full of documents belonging to the king, some of which were compromising. Soon the story of the secret box was being used by the king's enemies to reinforce their view of his guilt.

TRIAL AND EXECUTION

On 3 December, it was finally agreed that the king would stand trial before the Convention. The king made his first appearance on 11 December. He was charged with 'a multitude of crimes to establish your tyranny, thereby destroying liberty'. An account of the Revolution was read to him, interspersed with questions asking him to justify his actions. The king's replies were largely evasive, and although they did not incriminate him, they did not encourage confidence either.

BELOW *This engraving shows revolutionaries humiliating Louis XVI in the grounds of the Temple prison.*

The king made his second appearance on 26 December. This was followed in January by a series of votes to decide his fate. The deputies voted unanimously that Louis was guilty of conspiring against liberty and the safety of the state. A call for the king's punishment to be decided by the people in a referendum was rejected. And the third and crucial vote, on the death penalty, was carried by a majority of one. A final vote for mercy was defeated by 380 to 310, and the king went to the scaffold on 21 January 1793, where he was executed by guillotine.

BELOW *The king is executed by guillotine.*

Louis Capet (1754–93)

On the day that the Bastille was stormed, Louis XVI wrote one word to describe the day in his diary: 'Rien' – 'Nothing'. Some historians have seized on this as an illustration of the king's inability to cope with the events that overtook him, although what he actually meant was that he had not been hunting. He has often been portrayed as a dim-witted and bungling monarch. Yet there are other views of Louis Capet ('Louis the Last' as he was known at the end of his life), which show him as a far more sympathetic character, wanting to be loved by his people, but swayed at every turn by public opinion.

REVOLUTION IN THE COLONIES

When the Revolution started, France was still a major colonial power, and the jewel in its colonial crown was Saint-Domingue. This Caribbean island produced more than 40 per cent of the world's sugar and more than 50 per cent of its coffee. The French Atlantic ports, such as Bordeaux, La Rochelle and Nantes, had become spectacularly rich by importing sugar and coffee from the Caribbean, exporting manufactured goods to West Africa, and transporting slaves from West Africa to the Caribbean to work on the sugar and coffee plantations – the so-called 'Triangular Trade'.

The French colonies had royal governors. So, when Revolution broke out in France, the white landowners and merchants on Saint-Domingue tried to remove power from the governor. This prompted the island's mixed-race population, known as mulattos, to demand equality with the white population. In Paris, the National Assembly argued about what to do. On one side were deputies who were members of Les Amis des Noirs ('Friends of the Blacks'), an anti-slavery group; on the other were the powerful voices of the plantation owners and slave merchants.

In 1790, the mulattos rose against the white population of Saint-Domingue, but the revolt was suppressed and the mulattos' leader, Ogé, was executed. The following year there was a full-scale slave revolt on the island, in which Toussaint l'Ouverture emerged as a slave leader.

In 1793, France went to war with Britain and Spain (see page 42), both of whom were determined to seize valuable French colonial possessions. If the French colonies were to survive, the French now needed the co-operation of the non-white populations on the islands. The French National Convention therefore abolished slavery in France's colonies in February 1794. On hearing the news, Toussaint l'Ouverture came to the aid of the French, and his army of ex-slaves successfully fought the British and Spanish in Saint-Domingue.

? PEOPLE IN QUESTION

Toussaint l'Ouverture (1746–1803): a true revolutionary?

Toussaint l'Ouverture was often called the 'black Jacobin' (see page 42). He became known as l'Ouverture ('the Opening') because of his instinct for finding a way to break through enemy lines in battle. After driving out the Spanish and British, Toussaint took control of Saint-Domingue. He believed that, as part of the French Republic, the citizens of Saint-Domingue would at last be truly 'free and equal'. But, although France had abolished slavery, troops were sent to the island in 1802, under Napoleon (see page 51), to restore colonial rule. Toussaint l'Ouverture was captured and imprisoned in France where he died in 1803 from ill-treatment. Only a year later, the French were defeated in Saint-Domingue and the independent republic of Haiti was proclaimed.

LEFT *Toussaint l'Ouverture.*

BELOW *A Haitian folk painting, showing the Haitians defeating Napoleon's troops.*

CHAPTER 5

Terror and After

JACOBINS AND GIRONDINS

Many political clubs had sprung up during the early days of the Revolution. Leading members of the Jacobin Club (known as Jacobins) included Robespierre, Danton and Marat. Although there were Jacobin clubs all over France, 20 of the 24 Parisian deputies in the Convention were Jacobins. The Jacobins were therefore closely associated with the radical revolutionary politics of the capital and the *sans-culottes*. The name Girondins was given to a group of deputies who came from Bordeaux, capital of the Gironde in western France. They were suspicious of the power centred in Paris, and were more moderate than their Jacobin rivals.

RIGHT

A contemporary print showing the clothes worn by a typical Jacobin.

The trial and execution of Louis XVI (see pages 38–39) highlighted the deep political divisions within the National Convention. Those who thought that the king should not even have been allowed to stand trial were largely Jacobins. Those who called for a referendum to decide his punishment were mostly Girondins. There were also some deputies who belonged to neither of these two factions, but who voted with one group or the other depending upon the issue.

AFTER THE EXECUTION

Following the death of Louis XVI, France went to war with Britain, Holland and Spain. The French army needed more troops, so the Convention ordered 300,000 men to be conscripted. Attempts to enforce this conscription triggered open rebellion in the Vendée region of western France, where the rebels formed a 'Royal Catholic Army' dedicated to restoring the monarchy.

With foreign troops threatening France's borders and civil war raging in the west, the division between the two factions in the Convention became even deeper. On 2 June, the Jacobins bowed to intense pressure from the *sans-culottes* and had 29 Girondin deputies arrested.

This event stirred many more *départements* and cities across France into federalist revolts against Paris as the centre of power. Then, on 13 July, a Girondin sympathizer called Charlotte Corday stabbed Jean-Paul Marat to death while he was in his bath. Corday was sent to the guillotine four days later, and Marat was seen as a revolutionary martyr.

ABOVE *The Girondin deputies are arrested in 1793.*

? EVENT IN QUESTION

The Jacobin government: tyrants or social reformers?

The Jacobin government of 1793–94 is remembered largely for the killings during the Terror (see page 45), but many laws were passed during this time concerning social reform. These included a decree setting up a national system of public welfare, giving assistance to the poor, infirm and elderly; and a plan to provide free education for boys. Unfortunately, however, a shortage of money meant that these laws were not widely implemented.

THE COMMITTEE OF PUBLIC SAFETY

In April 1793, the crisis facing the National Convention forced the deputies to establish a Committee of Public Safety. This committee could pass decrees and make decisions about domestic and foreign defence. Its 12 members were drawn from the Convention, and they were re-elected every month.

In the summer of 1793, there was civil war (in the form of federalist revolts) throughout France, a continuing threat of foreign invasion, and a weakened economy. In Paris, the *sans-culottes* were a powerful force that could not be ignored by the Jacobin-led government. Meanwhile, members of the Committee of Public Safety worked night and day, determined to save the Revolution from failure. One member, Maximilien Robespierre, was to play a leading role in the next stage of the Revolution.

RIGHT *Leading Jacobin, Maximilien Robespierre.*

On 24 June, the Convention voted on a new Constitution, largely drawn up by Robespierre. It was very democratic, giving every male over 21 the right to vote. It also provided the right to state welfare and education, and the right to 'insurrection' if the government violated the people's rights. However, it gave individuals such wide-ranging freedoms that it had to be suspended straight away until the war ended.

THE TERROR

In early September, news reached Paris that the port of Toulon, in southern France, had been handed over by federalist supporters to the British navy. In the capital, the *sans-culottes* took to the streets, demanding more radical legislation against enemies of the Revolution, as well as higher wages and better food supplies. The Convention gave in to nearly all their demands, and a law was quickly passed authorizing the arrest of anyone who criticized the Revolution.

In the months that followed, thousands of people were imprisoned in Paris, and many were sent to the guillotine. Among them was the king's widow, Marie-Antoinette, and some of the Girondin deputies arrested in June. In the provinces, the Terror was even bloodier, as the rebellions were put down with great ferocity, particularly in the Vendée.

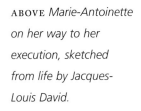

ABOVE *Marie-Antoinette on her way to her execution, sketched from life by Jacques-Louis David.*

? PEOPLE IN QUESTION

Maximilien Robespierre (1758–94): revolutionary hero or murderous tyrant?

Maximilien Robespierre trained as a lawyer, was greatly influenced by the writings of Jean-Jacques Rousseau (see pages 20–21), and became an active Jacobin. Known as 'the Incorruptible' because of his refusal to compromise with the king or his supporters, for many he was a hero of the Revolution. Yet for many others he was a murderous tyrant who tried to justify the mass killings of the Terror as being necessary to save the Revolution. He wrote: 'If the strength of popular government in peacetime is virtue, the strength of popular government in revolution is both virtue and terror; terror without virtue is disastrous, virtue without terror is powerless.'

ABOVE *Having looted Church property, the revolutionaries mock religion with a parade through Paris.*

DECHRISTIANIZATION

As the Terror continued, some deputies turned their attention to the Catholic Church, and a programme of 'dechristianization' was started. In the provinces, many churches and shrines were ransacked and closed down. All the churches in Paris were closed in November and Notre-Dame Cathedral was renamed the 'Temple of Reason'.

Meanwhile, the war effort continued and the French armies began to achieve some success. By spring 1794, there were no foreign armies in France, the civil war was over, and there was no effective opposition to the Committee of Public Safety. Yet the executions did not stop.

THE GREAT TERROR

On 10 June 1794, an infamous law was passed, speeding up the process of conviction. An accused person no longer had the right to a lawyer, and could now be convicted without any real evidence. In the 49 days that followed this decree, 1,400 men and women were executed in Paris (all provincial revolutionary courts had been closed down by the Committee in May). This time, until the fall of Robespierre, was known as the Great Terror.

THE FALL OF ROBESPIERRE

Distrust of Robespierre had been growing in the Convention for some time, with many deputies considering that he had become too powerful. The pressure of work had also taken its toll on Robespierre and his fellow Committee members and there were increasing disagreements. The end came on 27 July, after Robespierre had threatened to arrest various unnamed deputies. Instead Robespierre and his associates were them-selves arrested, and sent to the guillotine.

After this, the *jeunesse dorée* (or 'gilded youths') took to the streets of Paris and other major French cities. They were the sons and daughters of well-to-do prop-erty-owning families, and they delighted in taking revenge on the *sans-culottes*. For a while the Convention turned a blind eye to their activities. But the 'gilded youth' movement came to an end when Napoleon's troops put down the popular uprising in Paris on 5 October 1795 (see page 49).

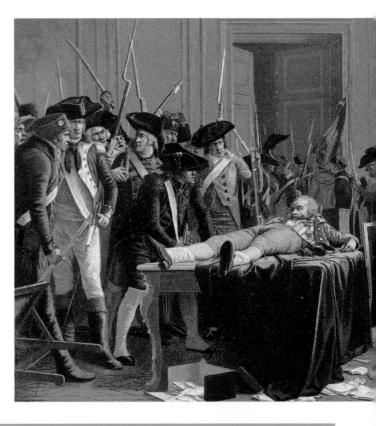

BELOW *Robespierre is wounded.*

(see page 49).

? EVENT IN QUESTION

Robespierre's overthrow: an end to Terror?

In the months following the overthrow of Robespierre, the Convention tried to steer the Revolution back on to a more moderate path. Prisoners were released, and the law of 10 June was repealed. But the violence did not end entirely. The Convention could not prevent a backlash against Jacobin supporters across the country. In Paris and other cities, the *jeunesse dorée* fought battles on the streets against the *sans-culottes*, while in the provinces royalist supporters took their revenge on their Jacobin persecutors in a time of killing called the 'White Terror'.

RESTORING THE MONARCHY

As the power of the *sans-culottes* declined, churches were allowed to reopen, the Convention took steps to rid the country of Jacobinism, and royalists began to talk once more about the restoration of the monarchy. Louis XVI's son, Louis-Charles, had been imprisoned in the Temple since the royal family was sent there in 1792. But any plans to put Louis XVII on the throne of France came to an end with the boy's death in June 1795. In July, Louis XVI's brother, the émigré Comte de Provence, unsuccessfully claimed his own succession to the throne as 'Louis XVIII'. A royalist attempt to invade Brittany, led by Louis' other émigré brother, and backed by the British, ended in failure and with the death of over 700 prisoners.

A NEW CONSTITUTION

The aim of the moderate deputies in the Convention was now to stabilize the Revolution. They began work on a new Constitution, to replace the suspended Constitution of 1793. The new Constitution removed many of the social rights provided by its predecessor, and the ownership of property once more became the basis of the right to vote. There would be two councils, and a governing Directory of five men appointed by one of the councils. In effect, the Constitution gave political and economic power back to well-to-do, middle-aged men. In order to preserve its own power, the Convention also decreed that two-thirds of the deputies in the new councils should be drawn from the ranks of the Convention itself.

BELOW *A member of the Convention, 1793.*

Although the Constitution was passed by a referendum, it was deeply unpopular. On 5 October, royalists tried to stir up opposition to the 'Law of Two-thirds' in Paris. The riots were put down by soldiers of the Convention, under the leadership of a young army officer called Napoleon Bonaparte.

LEFT *An engraving of the young Napoleon Bonaparte, Lieutenant of Artillery, after the painting by Jean-Baptiste Greuze.*

? WHAT IF...

a royal restoration had been successful?

In his declaration, the Comte de Provence committed himself to a return to the old regime if he sat on the throne of France as Louis XVIII. He referred to the restoration of the Three Estates and the power of the Church, as if there had been no Revolution at all. This uncompromising attitude meant that any real attempt to restore Louis XVIII to the throne would undoubtedly have torn the country apart in more civil war.

BONAPARTE (1769–1821)

As a member of a Jacobin club, Napoleon Bonaparte had been a supporter of the Revolution from the outset. He condemned the king's flight to Varennes, and was a friend of Maximilien Robespierre's brother, Augustin. After the downfall of Robespierre, Bonaparte came under suspicion as a Jacobin supporter, and was briefly imprisoned. However, the general in charge of the Convention troops in October 1795 had seen him in action, and knew what a talented army officer he was. He sent for Napoleon and asked him to serve him. From that moment, Bonaparte's career began to prosper once more.

FRENCH VICTORIES

Since 1792, France had been at war with much of Europe, but by the end of 1795 had either defeated, or negotiated peace with, all its enemies except for Britain and Austria. In 1796, the Directory put Napoleon in charge of an army on the Italian border with France. The idea was to drive the Austrians out of Italy, while another French army attacked Vienna more directly across the German border. In the end, however, Napoleon's army not only defeated the Austrians in Italy but almost reached the Austrian capital. Napoleon returned to Paris a hero.

BELOW *With fellow-Consuls Sieyès and Ducos, Napoleon takes possession of the Tuileries and seizes power in France, November 1799.*

When Britain continued to refuse to negotiate, the Directory decided to attack British commercial interests by threatening their trade with the Middle East and India. In May 1798, Napoleon set out for Egypt with about 38,000 men. But in August, the French were defeated by the British fleet under the command of Lord Horatio Nelson in the Battle of the Nile. Turkey and Russia entered the war, and Napoleon was stranded in Egypt. He defeated the Turks in July 1799, and then decided to return home, leaving the command of the French armies to a deputy. Once again, he was greeted in Paris as a victorious conqueror.

Napoleon knew that his country was tired of war and revolution. On 9 November, he seized power from the Directory and became First Consul of the Republic. The proclamation of the First Consul included the words: 'Citizens, the Revolution is established upon the principles which began it. It is over.'

ABOVE *Napoleon crowned himself emperor of France in 1804 (see page 58). Here he appears in his coronation robes.*

(see page 58).

> ### ❓ EVENT IN QUESTION
>
> ## *When did the Revolution end?*
>
> For Napoleon, the Revolution ended on 9 November 1799. But historians have long argued over when it really ended. They have also questioned whether the events from 1789 to 1799 can be labelled as a single 'Revolution', or if there were several stages of the Revolution in France. At each major turning point, members of the government would claim that the Revolution had run its course. But it seems that the Revolution only ended when some stability returned to the country – and this did not truly happen until Napoleon seized power.

CHAPTER 6

Views of the Revolution

FROM AMERICA

After the Fall of the Bastille in 1789, the Marquis de Lafayette (see page 17) sent the prison keys to George Washington, first president of the new United States of America, as a symbol of the triumph of liberty over oppression. There were many other links between the two countries, acknowledging the help

given by the French during the American Revolution (see pages 16–17). In August 1792, the French National Assembly voted to make three Americans – Washington, Alexander Hamilton and James Madison – honorary French citizens.

REVOLUTION AND AFTER

News of the Revolution in France was at first greeted with great enthusiasm in America. George Washington wrote in a letter of 1789: 'The Revolution which has been effected in France is of so wonderful a nature, that the mind can hardly recognize the fact...' One of the few early dissenting voices was that of John Adams, who was to become second president of the USA in 1797. But doubts became more widespread

ABOVE *George Washington (1732–99), first president of the United States.*

as news came of the execution of King Louis XVI, the September Massacres and the Terror.

In 1793, when France went to war with Britain (which had strong commercial links with America) relations between France and the USA became even more strained.

Nevertheless, the USA managed to remain neutral towards France, although feelings between the two countries soured as the 1790s drew to a close.

THE RIGHTS OF MAN

The author Thomas Paine was closely linked with both the American and French Revolutions. His book *The Rights of Man* was a response to a savage attack on the French Revolution written by the British statesman Edmund Burke (see page 54). *The Rights of Man*, published in two parts in 1791 and 1792, laid out the need for democratic government, as well as programmes for social welfare.

? **PEOPLE IN QUESTION**

BELOW *Thomas Paine.*

Thomas Paine: what role did he play?

Thomas Paine was born in England, but his fame is largely associated with a political pamphlet that he wrote after his arrival in America in 1774. *Common Sense* (1776) stated the cause of the American colonists and quickly became a bestseller. Fifteen years later, Paine published *The Rights of Man*. He was made a French citizen in 1792, and became a member of the National Convention. Despite speaking no French, he played a significant part in the life of the Convention – for instance, arguing convincingly, through an interpreter, against the execution of the king. He hoped to see the establishment of a French Republic based on the American model, but this dream was shattered after the Girondins fell from power. Paine was imprisoned by Robespierre but escaped the guillotine and was released after Robespierre's downfall.

FROM BRITAIN

In Britain, the events of 1789 at first met with general approval and enthusiasm. Some doubts began to be expressed as the Revolution lurched into violence, but the ideals expressed in the Declaration of the Rights of Man – Liberty, Equality, Fraternity – continued to generate huge excitement in Britain and across Europe. There was, however, one eloquent dissenting voice in Britain, speaking for those members of the Establishment who found the events in France deeply alarming. In 1790, Edmund Burke published *Reflections on the Revolution in France*, in which he attacked all aspects of the Revolution.

EDMUND BURKE (1729–97)

Burke was a member of the opposition Whig party in the British parliament. During the American Revolution he had openly criticized the British king, George III, and supported the cause of American liberty. However, he referred to the French crowds who took the Bastille as the 'swinish multitude', deploring what he called their 'barbarous philosophy'. Burke's main criticism was that the Revolution was trying to destroy the old institutions, rather than trying to reform them. He wrote: 'Kings will be tyrants from policy, when subjects are rebels from principle. When ancient opinions and rules of life are taken away, the loss cannot possibly be estimated. From that moment we have no compass to govern us.'

BELOW *Irish statesman and author Edmund Burke.*

Burke's *Reflections on the Revolution in France* sold 19,000 copies in six months, and his savage attack on the revolutionaries helped increase British distrust of the French. However, Thomas Paine's reply, *The Rights of Man* (see page 53), sold an amazing 200,000 copies in the same period, showing the interest of the time in the ideals that drove the French Revolution.

Once Britain went to war with France, any support for the French was seen as disloyalty to Britain and many British revolutionary sympathizers found themselves in a difficult position. As the war continued, the British government tried to encourage royalist risings within France, culminating in the failed attack on Brittany in 1795 (see page 48).

The Zenith of French Glory; _ The Pinnacle of Liberty.

? **PEOPLE IN QUESTION**

Thomas Carlyle's Revolution: fact or fiction?

The Scottish writer Thomas Carlyle (1795–1881) established his reputation with *The French Revolution: A History*, a mixture of fact and fiction, drawing on a wide variety of sources including eye-witness accounts, speeches, newspapers and memoirs, published in 1837. Carlyle had little sympathy for either the aristocrats of the old regime or for the revolutionaries. He wrote in a lurid style and described the Revolution as a time of chaos and violence. The book was very influential, and became the source and inspiration for Charles Dickens' novel, *A Tale of Two Cities*.

ABOVE *'The Zenith of French Glory' (c. 1792), a satirical cartoon by the English caricaturist James Gillray, shows the view of the French Revolution held by many people in Britain.*

IN EUROPEAN ART, MUSIC AND LITERATURE

The French Revolution was a major influence on European art, literature and music in the late eighteenth and early nineteenth centuries. In art, a new kind of painting emerged that celebrated the revolutionary ideals of liberty and democracy, often by looking back to the work of the ancient Greeks and Romans (Neoclassicism). In France itself, the official artist of the Revolution was Jacques-Louis David (1748–1825).

RIGHT *An engraving of the French painter and revolutionary, Jacques-Louis David.*

Many of his paintings portrayed revolutionary events and ideals. For example, after the murder of Jean-Paul Marat (see page 43), David painted a portrait of the stricken Marat, bleeding to death in his medicinal bath (1793). This painting drew on classical sculpture for its pose and its austere colouring, and portrayed Marat as a revolutionary martyr.

In Spain, Francisco de Goya was court artist to the king, but still sympathized with the revolutionary cause in France. When Napoleon's French troops occupied Spain in 1808, Goya and many others hoped that they would bring some revolutionary liberal ideals with them. But the brutality of the troops horrified the artist, and he reacted with one of his most famous paintings, *The Third of May 1808*, showing the execution of a group of Madrid citizens.

BRITISH POETS

'Bliss was it in that dawn to be alive...'
So wrote the British poet William Wordsworth about the dawn of Revolution in France. Both Wordsworth and the older Romantic poet William Blake were overjoyed at the early events of the French Revolution and looked forward to similar scenes in Britain. Wordsworth travelled in revolutionary France in the early 1790s, and sided with the Girondin faction in the Assembly. However, when the Jacobins took control of the government, and Robespierre began the Terror, Wordsworth felt that the ideals of the Revolution had been betrayed. He expressed his changing views in his long autobiographical poem *The Prelude*.

? **PEOPLE IN QUESTION**

Ludwig van Beethoven: a true revolutionary?

The German composer Ludwig van Beethoven was a revolutionary both in his music and in his politics. Despite relying on the patronage of wealthy aristocrats, he was fiercely independent, once declaring: 'There have been, and will be, thousands of princes. There is only one Beethoven.' His opera, *Fidelio*, celebrated the ideals of the French Revolution and he dedicated his Third Symphony to Napoleon, hero of Revolutionary France. However, when news came that Napoleon had proclaimed himself emperor, Beethoven felt that his hero had betrayed everything the Revolution stood for. He ripped out the title page from the symphony and wrote instead: 'Heroic Symphony, composed to celebrate the memory of a great man'. Yet, while Napoleon's actions may have seemed to many contemporaries to undermine the aims of the Revolution, by the time of his death he had made a return to the *ancien régime* in France an impossibility. Instead, France had become a modern nation state.

CHAPTER 7

The Legacy of the Revolution

What effect did a decade of change, instability, and civil and foreign war have on France? What was the legacy of the Revolution? These questions have been debated by historians ever since 1789.

The Revolution affected all levels of society. Many aristocrats lived in exile for years, only daring to return to France in the late 1790s. However the nobility began to recover under Napoleon. And, although aristocrats and nobles were never as powerful in France as they had been in pre-Revolution days, the aristocracy did survive.

The French Catholic Church, too, survived the attacks of the Revolution – although the wealth of the Church lands was gone forever. Most people had never given up their Catholic faith, and quickly returned to it once the churches reopened. However, the clergy had suffered: hundreds of priests went to the guillotine and thousands were exiled during the Revolution. Napoleon recognized the importance of the Church and made a settlement with the Catholic Church in 1801. The Revolution also brought freedom of worship to other religions in France, notably the French Protestants and Jews.

For ordinary people, the Revolution was mainly a time of turmoil. And after ten years, most people longed for the return of peace and stability. The group which gained most from the Revolution was probably the bourgeoisie, many of whom profited from land bought from émigré nobles and the Church.

Napoleon, the post-Revolution ruler, proved himself a brilliant military leader. France's armies swept across Europe in the early nineteenth century and, in 1804, Napoleon crowned himself emperor of the French. However, after military defeat in Spain and Portugal, and then in Russia, he was exiled to the

Italian island of Elba. For a brief period Louis XVI's brother, the Comte de Provence, returned to the French throne. But Louis XVIII was forced to flee when Napoleon returned in triumph to Paris. Napoleon was finally defeated at the Battle of Waterloo in 1815, and died in exile on St Helena in 1821.

ABOVE Liberty Leading the People, *painted by Eugène Delacroix in 1830.*

? **EVENT IN QUESTION**

The French Revolution: triumph or tragedy?

The events of 1789 have been interpreted in many different ways. For some historians, the French Revolution was a triumph for ordinary people, who were not to blame for the violence it unleashed. For others, the Revolution started well but turned sour when the violence began. For still others, the upheavals and killings of the Revolution were all part of a tragic episode. However, it is generally agreed that the French Revolution was a turning point in world history. The events in France allowed people to think in new and 'revolutionary' ways, and inspired later uprisings all around the world – for example in 1848, when there were revolutions across much of Europe, and in 1917, when the Russian people finally brought imperial rule to an end in their country.

Timeline

1756–63
Seven Years' War.

1770
Marriage of dauphin (future Louis XVI) and Marie-Antoinette.

1774
Louis XVI becomes king.

1775–83
American War of Independence.

1776
American Declaration of Independence.
Necker joins the French government.

1781
Necker resigns, and is succeeded by Calonne.

1787
Meeting of Assembly of Notables.

1789
MAY: Meeting of the Estates-General.

17 JUNE: Third Estate declares the National Assembly.

20 JUNE: Tennis Court Oath.

23 JUNE: Royal Session.

11 JULY: Louis XVI sacks Necker.

14 JULY: Fall of the Bastille.

LATE JULY: Time of the 'Great Fear'.

11 AUGUST: Decree of abolition of feudalism and special privileges of the nobility.

26 AUGUST: National Assembly passes the 'Declaration of the Rights of Man and of the Citizen'.

5 OCTOBER: March of marketwomen to Versailles.

NOVEMBER: Church property nationalized.

1790
14 JULY: Feast of the Federation.

27 NOVEMBER: Decree ordering clergy to take oath of obedience.

1791
20 JUNE: Royal family captured at Varennes.

AUGUST: Slave rebellion in Sainte-Domingue.

27 AUGUST: Declaration of Pillnitz.

14 SEPTEMBER: Louis XVI accepts Constitution.

1 OCTOBER: First meeting of the Legislative Assembly.

1792
20 APRIL: France declares war on Austria.

30 JULY: Marseille *fédérés* enter Paris.

10 AUGUST: Storming of Tuileries Palace; overthrow of monarchy.

1 SEPTEMBER: Prussians capture Verdun, leading to September Massacres in Paris.

20 SEPTEMBER: First meeting of the National Convention.

21 SEPTEMBER: Abolition of the monarchy.

22 SEPTEMBER: France declared a republic.

11 DECEMBER: Start of the trial of the king.

1793
21 JANUARY: Execution of the king.

MARCH: Start of revolt in Vendée.

APRIL: Committee of Public Safety created.

2 JUNE: Arrest of the Girondin deputies.

24 JUNE: New Constitution passed, then immediately suspended.

13 JULY: Murder of Marat.

SEPTEMBER ONWARDS: Time of the Terror.

16 OCTOBER: Execution of Queen Marie-Antoinette.

NOVEMBER: Time of dechristianization; all churches in Paris closed.

1794
4 FEBRUARY: Abolition of slavery in French colonies.

27 JULY: Arrest of Robespierre.

28 JULY: Execution of Robespierre.

1795
JUNE: Death of 'Louis XVII'.

Royalists land in Brittany.

5 OCTOBER: Napoleon's troops put down popular uprising on the streets of Paris.

NOVEMBER: Directory takes office.

1796
Napoleon takes command in Italy.

1798
Napoleon goes to Egypt.

1799
9 NOVEMBER: Napoleon seizes power from the Directory.

Glossary

absolute monarchy A political system in which all power lies with the monarch.

ancien régime The term used by revolutionaries for the political system before 1789.

Assembly of Notables In pre-revolutionary France, a group of nobles, *intendants*, magistrates, clergy and others, all chosen by the king.

bourgeoisie Wealthy people who did not have the status or privileges associated with the nobility, for example doctors, lawyers, bankers, merchants and manufacturers.

cahiers de doléances Lists of grievances submitted by people across France before the meeting of the Estates-General in 1789.

counter-revolutionaries People who opposed the Revolution.

decree A statement of law.

départements The 83 administrative regions into which France was divided in 1790.

émigrés People who left France on political grounds during the Revolution.

Enlightenment An eighteenth-century philosophical movement that emphasized the use of reason.

federalist Supporter of federalism, a political system favoured by the Girondins.

fédérés Military volunteers who came to Paris from the provinces to celebrate the first Fête de la Fédération on 14 July 1790, and again in 1792.

First Estate In pre-revolutionary France, the clergy.

généralités The 33 regions into which the whole of pre-revolutionary France was divided for administrative purposes.

Girondins The name given to a group of deputies who came from Bordeaux, capital of the Gironde in western France. They were more moderate than their Jacobin rivals.

intendants In pre-revolutionary France, ministers appointed by the king who were responsible for tax collection and public works in the *généralités*.

Jacobins Members of the Jacobin Club, who became associated with the radical revolutionary politics of Paris and the *sans-culottes*.

jeunesse dorée ('gilded youths') Sons and daughters of well-to-do, property-owning families who attacked Jacobins and militant *sans-culottes* after the fall of Robespierre.

métayage (share-cropping) A system of tenancy in which the landlord took a share of crops from the tenant in the place of cash rent.

National Guard The revolutionary militia formed after the fall of the Bastille.

noblesse d'épée People whose noble status could be traced back over many generations.

noblesse de robe People whose noble status came from their position in the royal bureaucracy.

parlements in pre-revolutionary France, the high courts of the 13 judicial districts.

philosophes A group of Enlightenment thinkers in France that included Rousseau, Voltaire, Diderot and Montesquieu.

refractories Clergy who refused to take the oath of obedience to the state demanded in 1791.

remontrance in pre-revolutionary France, a formal objection to proposed laws made by the courts to the king.

Salic Law An ancient law that barred women from succession to the throne.

sans-culottes ('without breeches') Craftsmen, shopkeepers and labourers who took part in militant revolutionary activity.

Second Estate In pre-revolutionary France, the nobility.

seigneurs In pre-revolutionary France, lords who had various rights and privileges dating from the medieval feudal system such as hunting and shooting rights, and the right to keep pigeons.

Third Estate Everyone in pre-revolutionary France who was not part of the nobility or the clergy, from peasants to the bourgeoisie.

Further information

BOOKS

Richard Cobb, Colin Jones, *The French Revolution: Voices from a Momentous Epoch 1789–1795* (Simon and Schuster, 1988)

Sean Connolly, *Witness to History: The French Revolution* (Heinemann Library, 2003)

William Doyle, *The Oxford History of the French Revolution* (Oxford University Press, 1980)

Origins of the French Revolution (Oxford University Press, 1980)

Hugh Gough, *Studies in European History: The Terror in the French Revolution* (Macmillan, 1998)

Christopher Hibbert, *The Days of the French Revolution* (Penguin, 1989)

Colin Jones, *Longman Companion to the French Revolution* (Longman, 1988)

Peter McPhee, *The French Revolution 1789–1799* (Oxford University Press, 2002)

Stewart Ross, *Events and Outcomes: The French Revolution* (Evans, 2002)

Simon Schama, *Citizens: A Chronicle of the French Revolution* (Penguin, 1989)

Mark Steel, *Vive La Révolution* (Scribner, 2003)

NOTE ON SOURCES

A source is information about the past. Sources can take many forms, from books, films and documents to physical objects and sound recordings.

There are two types of source, primary and secondary. Primary sources date from around the time you are studying; secondary sources, such as books like this, have been produced since that time. In general, primary sources are more accurate but contain much narrower information than secondary sources.

Here are some guidelines to bear in mind when approaching a written or drawn source:

1. Who produced it (a politician, cartoonist, etc?) and why? What was their motive? Were they trying to make a point?

2. When exactly was the source produced? What was going on at the time? Detail is key here, not just the year but sometimes even down to the exact time of day.

3. Might the source have been altered by an editor, censor or translator? (Possible change in translation is very important.)

4. Where was the source produced? Which country, town, region, etc?

5. Does the source tie in with other sources you have met, primary and secondary, or does it offer a new point of view?

6. Where has the source come from? Has it been selected by someone else (probably to prove a point – beware!) or did you find it through your own research? The only valid primary sources are those uncovered in genuine research.

Index

Numbers in **bold** refer to pictures.